Mind your Manners In School

Arianna Candell / Rosa M. Curto

BARRON'S

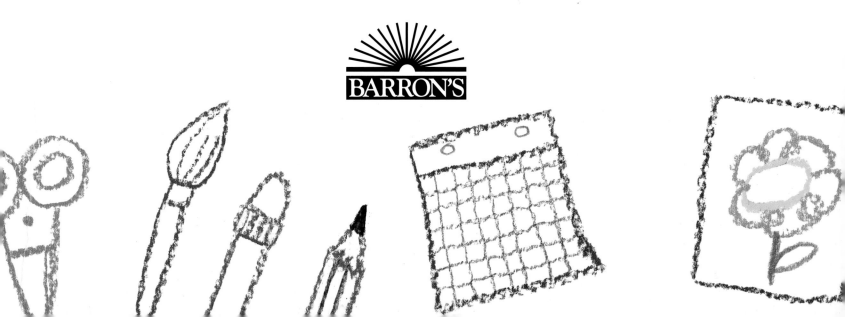

Back to school

John is going to a new school, but he doesn't want to go. He tells his mother that he doesn't know his classmates, his teacher, or his new classroom. Ann, a girl in his class, sees that John is very sad. She meets him outside the school and takes his hand. Ann and John soon become close friends.

Be an early bird

Ann is an early bird and is always first to arrive at school. Peter, however, is often late. Snuggled under his blankets, he has a hard time getting up. Then he thinks of his waiting classmates,
and he jumps up!
Are you an early bird?

Learn to be patient

Today the children are learning to work with clay. Peter is making some awesome animals that never break! Laura is not as patient as Peter. She looks upset and just can't get started. Peter sees this and offers to help her. Now she's happy with the clay figure she's making.

Washing your hands

Playing on the playground is so much fun! The children play ball, jump rope, and play with sand. When they go back to the classroom, all the kids must wash their hands. Ann doesn't like to wait in line. Sometimes she goes straight back to her place at the table. Laura reminds her to clean her hands or she may get their books and school supplies dirty.

Learning to share

The toys at school are for everyone, and classmates should share them. Norah's older brother always lets her borrow his box of colored pencils. However, when Norah brings some storybooks to school, she doesn't want to let anyone borrow them. When she realizes that her classmates like to read new stories as much as she does, she finally shares her books.

Everybody, play!

When games are played in the playground or classroom, the more people who play, the better! Paul and Lucy especially enjoy playing ball, and they want several kids to play with them. They both know that it's more fun to include everyone. That's why all the children at their school get a chance to play.

Is everybody ready?

Today the children will paint a picture to take home. They can't begin because
Mary is still walking around. Everyone must be seated and ready before they
can start. Martin has to call her to sit next to him. Then, at last, she rushes
to her seat!

Quiet! Quiet!

Quiet!

It has been several days since school started, and John is feeling better about school every day. He has so many friends and so many things to talk about! He talks even when he should listen to the teacher or work quietly. This bothers his classmates who want to hear what the teacher has to say. They often have to ask John to be quiet and pay attention.

That's not funny

It isn't easy to say who likes to
kid around the most in class,
but David and Rachel surely
like to tease their classmates!
They often make jokes that
are not always funny.
Sometimes their jokes
are cruel, and they
are the only ones
who laugh. Jokes
are only funny
when everyone
can enjoy them.

Pick up and clean up

We all know that after playing and working, it's time to pick up and clean up. Pick up toys and wastepaper after cutting, clean your brushes after using paints, and put away your supplies.

We all know this, but don't always do it. In John's class, they had a good idea. Every day, one classmate makes sure everyone helps to keep the classroom clean. Today, it's Adrian's turn.

Helping each other

How high can you count? Did you know that even if we wanted to, we could never finish counting? Numbers are infinite. That means that they continue forever. Paul and Norah have a great time playing with numbers. Lucy and David find math a little difficult.

Since the four of them are friends, they help one another. This makes their work seem easier, so math is more fun!

Let's talk about it

Do you think that kids who hit other kids are stronger and braver?

Peter doesn't. He explains to Laura that these kids haven't learned to solve their problems by talking. He knows that words can help to make friends, so he pushes fighters away.

If you have fights often, try to find solutions by talking, like Peter does.

You're lucky!

John, Ann, Peter, Norah, Paul, Lucy, Mary, Martin, David, Rachel, and Adrian are about to finish school. They have learned to live together with their group. They respect and help one another, and this is as important as all the learning they accomplish. They are very lucky because they have learned to share so much together.

Everyone is different

As you have seen, not everyone likes to do the same things. Some can draw very well, and others can read or do math well. We can help one another by sharing our talents.

No two people are exactly alike, and that's why we can always learn something from someone else.

Activities

LISTENING FOR SILENCE

In this activity, you must be absolutely quiet. No one can make any kind of noise. Everyone sits in place for one minute to listen to silence.

During this time, you will hear noises. Someone may move a chair, a car outside may honk its horn, or thunder may boom in the sky.

You will discover that during this silent minute, not everyone will have heard the same noises. Remember to listen very carefully.

CLASSROOM GAMES

When we have finished our work, the teacher sometimes lets us play. We love to play a game in which we hide an object and then find it.

Someone is chosen to hide something small in the classroom. The rest of the children cover their eyes. The children must find the object without leaving their places, so it can't be completely hidden. The game is to find it by just using your eyes!

The child who finds it gets to hide the next object.

Another game shows how good your memory is! Eight or ten objects are chosen and placed on a table. Everyone looks at them for a short time. Then they are covered with a piece of cloth.

Players take turns naming one of the objects under the cloth. The game is over when no one can remember what was there or when everything has been guessed.

THE OBSTACLE COURSE

Do you remember that we talked about all of the kids playing together? The more who play, the more fun it is. Pay attention then, and start having fun with your friends. Are you ready?

An adult can help you prepare a race with obstacles. In this kind of race, you don't have to run in a straight line. Instead, you have to run and avoid obstacles you find in the way.

You might use some empty buckets turned upside down. Separate them enough so you can zigzag between them. When you get to the end, return to the start and then jump over each obstacle. Which way was the fastest?

TAKING ATTENDANCE

Everyday, someone in the class is responsible for taking attendance to check that everyone is present. Today we will suggest a new and funny way of checking who's in school. Cut out as many rectangular pieces of cardboard as there are students in the class. Each student then writes his or her name using green on the front and red on the back of the cards.

The teacher can help you put the cards in alphabetical order, and then you can pin the cards to the classroom bulletin board following the same order.

Everyday, a different boy or girl will be in charge of reading the names. If everyone is present, the roll call will be all green, but if someone is missing, his or her name will appear in red. Don't you think this is a good way to take attendance? This will really help the teacher.

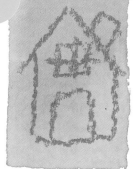   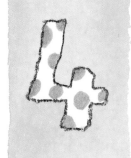 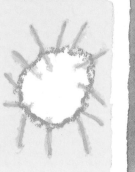 

Guidelines for parents

GOING TO SCHOOL

The first section may help your child to understand that going to school may seem difficult at first. Explain that going to school helps children get ready for adult life. Talk about all the exciting things that will be done in the classroom. Some of their early class friendships may last a lifetime.

Also emphasize that being able to go to school is actually a privilege. There are many children who cannot attend school even if they would like to. In many countries, children must work or take care of younger brothers and sisters. They don't have the chance to learn how to read, write, draw, and do so many other activities.

LET'S TALK ABOUT IT!

We know that most children have fights. It's still up to us to discourage violence by teaching our children how to solve problems by talking with others. Explain that not everyone will want to be our friend. However, we can still use words to try to solve our differences. We should also explain how important it is to admit that we have made a mistake. Learning to apologize is the most important lesson in repairing relationships.

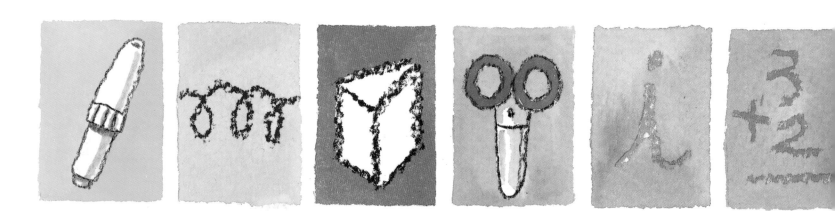

HELP!

In one of the sections, we saw that Laura had difficulty making clay figures. Arnie was quick to help her. This positive attitude should be emphasized as you read the story aloud. It is very endearing to see our children cooperating and helping one another. We should also stress that no one does everything perfectly or is good in every activity. We can encourage children to know how to help and also to ask for help when needed. There is always someone willing to lend a hand.

GETTING THINGS DONE

We discussed the importance of getting up and being ready for school. Also remind your child not to postpone tasks. It's so important to be punctual and to be on time so that others don't have to wait. Being prompt will be important throughout life. Parents must be on time for work and children must be on time for school. Even very young children should understand that they have duties and must be responsible.

CLEAN AND TIDY

There are many children who do not like to tidy up or believe it's not important to have clean hands. Ask these children if they would like to live in a very messy home, or if they would like their parents to fix and eat dinner with dirty hands. We can provide strong role models for children so that they will reflect our actions rather than those of others.

Children should also be taught early on that it's important that they help keep their classrooms and play areas neat. If everyone pitches in and helps put things away, tidying up will go much faster. And, everyone benefits since toys and supplies are put back where they belong and where they can be easily found by all.

Parents should encourage this spirit of cooperation and the need for neatness at home. Young children enjoy taking part in family chores and helping mom and dad. In the process, they develop a feeling of self-worth, which can carry them into adulthood.

Original title of the book in Catalan: *Com ens hem de comportar a l'Escola*
© 2005 Gemser Publications, S.L.
Author: Arianna Candell
Illustrator: Rosa M. Curto

All inquiries should be addressed to:
Barron's Educational Series, Inc.
250 Wireless Boulevard
Hauppauge, New York 11788
www.barronseduc.com

International Standard Book No. 0-7641-3166-4

Library of Congress Catalog Card No. 2004111321

Printed in China
9 8 7 6 5 4 3

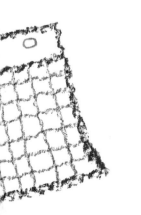